The Ages of Water

Books by Walter Perrie

POETRY

A Lamentation for the Children 1977
By Moon and Sun 1980
Concerning the Dragon 1984
From Milady's Wood 1997
Decagon: Selected Poems 1995-2005
Lyrics & Tales in Twa Tongues 2010

PROSE

Out of Conflict: Essays 1982
Roads that Move: A Journey through Eastern Europe 1991

The Ages of Water

Poems by
Walter Perrie

Grace Note Publications

The Ages of Water
This edition published 2020 by
Grace Note Publications C.I.C
Grange of Locherlour,
Ochtertyre, PH7 4JS,
Scotland

books@gracenotereading.co.uk

ISBN 978-1-913162-12-2

First Published in 2020

copyright © Walter Perrie 2020

A catalogue record for this book is available
from the British Library

"Raconte-t-on jamais autre chose que sa propre histoire?"
Philippe Besson

for TREVOR ROYLE

Dreaming another Scotland
future history
recast in an ancient foundry
alloy of people, stories, land.

ACKNOWLEDGEMENTS

Marie Stuart appeared in the annual Bulletin of the Franco-Scottish Society for 2017-18.

Plea for a Healing appeared in *Vigils*, Fras, 2015.

Earlier versions of some poems from *The Ages of Water* appeared as *Sorceries*, Fras, 2018.

Over many years my friend Robin Magowan, poet, traveller and gardener, has been generous not only with encouragement but with sharp-eyed comment on a number of these poems.

CONTENTS

A Riddle from Before the Flood

Cloud-hidden the fastness behind you,
source of your hope and sorrows,
days of luminous delight, tomorrows
black with love-despair; you
grope your way away from me
but never leave, unscaleable; from me
your snowmelt sweetens the sea.
Who am I?

Quanta

Blur in the mist
the roebuck stood
long motionless
waiting for me to pass
as vaguely I would.

Birth

Blood-smeared, slime-slippy, hungry
whelp, howling your neediness:
clean me, feed me, keep me warm.
Wide-innocent eyes;
cunning, manipulative, wise.

Infant

Tempest, Wars, the World
rants and roars and quietly
pours itself into
the cradle where you lie
and space and time are filled
with dream, and you
in your dreaming turn and sigh
– and all is stilled.

Speech I

The first astounded him, stumbled out without him
knowing how, then another, the forced shape
strange; the long soft lips-together *mmmm*,
the out-breath hisses *esss, efff*, the puffs *ttt, ppp*;
mama, mamasha. Hard, welding the bits together:
no, bye, sky, look, mine, man, tree, first singly, then
straggling few by few; *come-in, want-go, down-there,*
give-me, hungry, want-water, play-garden.
Visitors came unsummoned – wanting attracts
them – families of verbs with hangers-on, structure bits,
disciplined companies, regiments with facts
and skills, well-ordered drills, relentless rules, what fits
with what. Even the poor subjunctive till he knew
he had them under control, mastered them – finally!

Speech II

Then it began to go wrong, not obvious at first,
little deceptions, disappointments, empty space
between the promise and the gift, a niggling thirst
left unassuaged, a lover plays false, disgrace
like a secret punishment. And what can get said
was all he could say; tricked into keeping them,
the sticky lies, unspoken silences betrayed,
pre-dawn disappearances he could not condemn,
feelings awry, dream things he could not identify.
Too late, ignoring him, they staged their coup,
blatant, by day. Now he knew, no need for tanks; *We
were complicit, phrase by phrase, nothing we could do....*
Many were taken, whole peoples, men, women,
children, not heard from again.

What Loiters

Fear the night woods, the unknown,
unsayable, something haunts
the hedgerow, haunts the witch wood;
run the long, dark louring arc,
watching hawthorn, muttering oak.

Desolate of wolf and bear, Great Caledon
shelters nothing now to fear more than
what loiters in the human dark.

Ténèbres

1

The field is bare, no love grows here;
the birch without hope, the stream
a ruin of black dismay;
here is neither space nor time,
only the blinding fogs; the boy
in his unutterable cell
has no star nor moon for friend,
but bitter snow, an empty wind
and Soul soliciting an end.

2

Shell-sheltered in yolk-yellow whin
he hearkens to the winter wind:
the wind says;
Let me in, I am Time,
and the whin says;
I am Flower and Stem;
and the pine-top sways
to the wind and says;
I am Endurance, let me in.

And the rains begin.

Boy

Across your spirit-haunted sea,
uncharted yet, some foreign hand
steers you as far-near to the reef
as the death you do not yet foresee
and in a spasm sharp as grief –
a clear blue outline – liveable land!

Topography

Wide, wider with each day the sea,
shore-life a misting memory,
only some infant peaks remain
to pierce the cloud, unearthly;
uncertain smile, a tune,
unknowable topography.

Test

"Throw mure and moss, throw banké, busk, and breir."
                                                Henryson

Dungavel, fourteen, a chilly-wet
thin-windy February day to make my way,
a week-end scout, with compass-map
to Loudoun Hill and back, by black burn-spate,
farm fence-barb, bog: *Take apple, cheese,*
water. Be back by dark! Don't be late!
Loudoun Hill, the first of Bruce's victories!
Wherever I go, forever up to my knees
in peat-bog bloody histories.

Family Gatherings

At each Sunday dinner father
would polish his repertoire of complaint;
That's too much salt. Sit straight! Insolent
ingrate, who do you think pays for
your food, your clothes? Many a poor
boy would be glad of your waste.
No, you may not rise from table. Haste
will be your ruin. What you don't eat
will be on your breakfast plate.
Unforgettable, father's lessons: how to hate
family gatherings.

Youth

Youth in thrall to your new-found force:

My truth, my strength, my Will prevails,
unquenchable, due west or south, my sails
full-spread thrill ahead;
before me a dazzle-course
of days, free of my dead
wake, old uncertainties.

Will and Desire are ice and fire;
burn or freeze – your gods – you choose.

Deirdre's leaving of Scotland

Short, short are our days in Scotland;
Glen Etive, Glendaruel
loch-scattered fairyland
green and gold.

Out of our bitter Ireland fled,
each binding the other
in fate's love-net
black, white, red.

Grey mossy stone in Glen Etive
made our first shelter, bracken
slopes a cattle-fold
herding the sun.

In steep, deep-wooded Glen Massan
half-sleeping we listen
to clarsach-tunes
on the burn.

Wake up to green-gold mornings, chill
in lark-light, walk the dream
pastures of may-thorn
rowan, broom.

Ever, ever I would stay there
but you would not stay, not stay
to hear the *cuckoo, cuckoo*
fade away.

Glen Etive, Glen Orchy, Dun Súibhne
green Glendaruel, slow, weighty
names as honey
coat my tongue.

I would not leave you, Scotland,
but to go with my love
sweet-voiced Naoise
hand in hand;

he of the raven-hair
brow of the snow-drift
mouth of blood.

Three Matches

For a glimpse of your face
I strike one match, one more
for your sparkle eyes,
and the last, sad light
in my cradle-hands
to memorise the prize.

Resilience

As this leaf falls
the fresh wound seals
the scarred wood waits
another spring.

Glen Etive

Glen Etive deep
in dreaming snow
remembers the track
we wandered
an ancient spring ago.

Gorse and Yew

Gets harder weathering winter on Scottish winter;
survivors grow a thick resilience of soul. Through
flood, snow, frost, gale, sun, hail,
grandfather oaks and beeches fail.
Hard as rage, in grudging age, the yew
survives from cemetery stock made new.

One night, rime-bright in starlight, the sheep
lay gem-like a-glitter. Without remorse
God nets life-heat in bitter webs, the weep
and beautiful warp of things and Scotland's gorse
blooms gowden-gay, prickles the January frost
with scattergood sun-blossom, careless of cost.

Calligraphy

Cool water-script, the westering geese
brush *Morning* on a taut blue
silk, signing with swift sure
strokes a spring departure, and their few
remembered calls the only trace
we were ever here.

Dunnock

In camouflage browns and greys,
featherlight under the bushes,
hop-about, peck-about, discreet,
your days are archaic adventure;
sex, territory, victory, defeat:
flitting through the leaf detritus
go Helen, Achilles, Hector.

All Things are Signs

Some differences the tribe will tolerate,
some not. Mother's mother's sage-femme mother:
a birth; a tail, smothered and buried late
by moonlight. Deformities, other
curse-blessings of a demon-god are perilous,
hazard soul-pollution. Thin-skinned to difference,
the old are most at risk: *Purge our offence!*
Let what sent it say Life or Death, not us!

Dissident sexualities, shaman-eagle, woman-man
with drum and due precaution, unsettle
orders of Earth and Heaven, pluck a petal
from blossom grows where no mortal human
goes, pacify the demon-gods, say what beware,
what sacrifice or where the pilgrimage must go.
Not bound to one sense, the Different declare:
all things are signs for those who care;
                    as above, so below.

A Gaelic Air

Weighted with generations the fiddle soars
from C to A with a swerve of bow;
pale congregations mass behind the tune,
intone the great sea-swelling psalms;
retreat, resurgence, hope and woe.

This Startled Hare

This startled hare is gift and grace
to start my heart-beat fresh, to brace
me to his pace as off we race
with lope-leap-streak, black ear-tips up
to leap long feather-grasses: stop,
sniff-whiff the early air; at play
life's trick in body-soul: praise-pray
such goodly gifts this godly day.

Suleiman the Magnificent

after Titian

To honour an ancestor
Suleiman, known to Venice
as *Il Gran' Signor*,
ordains
in one palm-sheltered place:
rose gardens,
wells, bazaar,
public baths, library,
school, mosque, soup kitchen to feed
the poor, a caravanserai,
hospital, a hospice
where a Man might die
with dignity. What more?

On the Hill

The horizon you carry always with you
lays you back in the buzz-busy heather,
dissolves in your sky-spinning weather
and worlds. Our gravity is the way
light bends us round its flicker-day.

See Earth with her mystery,
prodigal of whatever we may be,
unfold our time like a flower
open at once in all its stages,
impassioned nights, days, water ages,
our tidal seed-leaf-blossom-death,
             over and over.

Ambition

You say you want to *Be* yourself, *Own*
a life? Did you abandon
who you might have been
for who they wanted you to seem?
Not handsome, clever, even
good enough? Was it easier?
There were pleasures to be had here,
nights out, the pub, TV, money enough.
Say then; the dream was a snare,
wire at your neck, you caught there
forever, squealing your dream-stuff.

Black-Letter Language

Kraa... kraa... kraa... kraa... you shout,
defending your territory. But I say:
cacophonous, ink-stinky crow
perched along the winter branches, bleak
shifty letters in a gothic font, woe-
bringer on a painted sky, black-
hearted conspirator, spell-spinner I call
you; eye-pecking carrion-feeder, hoodie,
crack-tongued as a broken angel
with all your bitter truths to tell.

Scarecrow

Line the fence-wire with a row
of corvid corpses. They read our post;
We too have terrible things to say:
lexicons, grammars, warrants of arrest,
I name You so and so... fit to be blesst,
I pronounce You... exile. You.... go free.

Well named these sentences,
doom-dealers we invent.
No spell nor prayer can relent
what nails us to our triple cross;
absence, presence, *consequence*;
two thieves and a Christ in the middle.

Methven Moss

Under Methven Moss or Dupplin
Scot and English lie as one:
cross and crescent, flag and banner
brave the skies as cities burn.

The Dunning runs down to the Earn,
the Earn runs into the Tay,
and all the while the seas and stars
whisper of eternity.

Silence the Poor

Just a wee operation to take out your sense
of purpose-worth. Just relax now, you won't feel
anything really, just an intense
listlessness. Amazing, how soon you will heal.

Silence the poor!

Those for whom charity is a daily scar,
whose humanity is hammered shut
with gilded nails, who learn to endure
nothing, not damage their cages or shout
too much. Those for whom the deck is stacked
by card-sharps, dealers, folk they respect.

Surplus, you will be exposed at birth or soon after
to profitable life, not on a bare Attic hill but where
nor gods nor dryads shall bear witness nor wolf care
for you. We shall say you were never really here.

The Cry

All wars are the same war, over and over,
only the incidentals change, location,
how long the truce, *combien de morts?*
The generations each betray their own;
the Somme, Gettysburg, Marathon,
and the same sad cry from the cross.

Lizard

Startled, he freezes, mottled lemon-green
against the wall: *I am dead, unmoving thing*
poised on the relentless edge of living.
Close-to, I see the pulse of belly-throat,
my co-conspirator; he will not
blink though the stakes be high as heaven.

Mathematician, measuring mass
against compulsive inner joy, secret
behind a stony gaze, a stillness
holding fast to what he is, incarnate
hungers, triumph of animate
light, pulse configuring chaos.

Marsyas

after Titian

A speaker of truths to power – sad fool:
triangle of inverted limb, dead weight
the viol mocks; an old man looks on; caught
in time a little lapdog laps the pool
of blood drips from the flesh already flayed.
Curious Apollo with a little blade
investigates, repelled by the hairiness, the smell.
The god of measure does not bow to pain
or happiness, symmetrically beautiful
he cloaks his tricks in prohibitive reason,
disguise of all unreasonable gods; abstract
indifference measures the right and wrong
of life by number, syllable, raw fact
where all our mess and tenderness belong.

In campagna

First light, ant regiments haul away
history; yesterday's scorpion corpse.

Noon shimmer-trembles, cicadas play
sticks and rattles in the underbrush.

Gloaming timpani, cymbals crash;
a great black storm-bull charges the mountain.

Moon gets up from her house by the stream,
her sanctus bell silvers leaf-litter
of lovers millennia deep.

Back-lit, serene, the night-woods oboe and flute
till a bird-people pipe from the bushes,
bats and the night people sleep.

Pulcinella: *aria for a politician*

Recitative:

Ageless, middle-aged, paunchy, raunchy,
long-nosed, a hump-back debauchee,
Prince Universal, I am He
self-made Lord of the bad, sad, sane,
mad master of all I see –
saving, naturally, your good selves, for I remain,
My Public Dear, your humble servant.
When don't I get you what you want?

Chorus: allegretto vivace;

Too busy a pander to ponder too long,
I entertain everyone just with a song:
the unpleasant peasants, the work-harried proles,
aristo peacocks who're through to their souls,
bourgeois defenders of all that's their own,
junkies and punkies, the foreigner monkeys,
scroungers and loungers, dafties and drunkies
the work-shy, the crippled and poverty prone.

Love again

Invisible forces
spur the sea; a sight of you,
these white sea-horses
crest and crash – tsunami.

Love who you will

Three crow-crones on a crooked branch
warn against love with black dismay.
Love who you will, defy their shrill
      crowcophony.

Edinburgh Gifts

Dawn shutters disclose chiaroscuro
mist on The Meadows;
in our honour her trees
put on cherry-blossom kimonos
and a generous sun bestows
a necklace of golden windows.

I like when

I like when you lend me your openness;
lets me slip artless
through barb and bramble
me to you.

I like when you tell me *I missed you,*
your sensuality
sure of its pleasure
in we two.

I like when you lend me your eyes,
mirrors flung open
bending perspective
to see me.

I like when you lend me your tongue
wordless translator
transgressing semantics
to say you.

Hirundo rustica

Honour the lively, fleet-winged *hirondelle*,
rondine, pool-skimmer, dust-bather, here-gone
diver-dodger, streamer-trailing interceptor,
barn-lodger acrobat, bright-feathered bagatelle
master of high-sky marathon.

Bold bundle of purposes, you feed
swing-winging desert, ocean, jungle, wood;
fat farmlands roll below you; master-mason, shape-
creator, mud-hut maker, feeding fledglings,
season-setter, summoning the weather-scape
you want, turning the world under your wings.

Muse

1

Jaguar sleek, His hair all rainbow,
eyes as cobalt, heart as the moons go,
      changeable.

Should you meet Him, all is lost;
a day without Him is a waste;
parasite or godly guest,
        ineffable

2

Who I wanted went away,
life suspended.
My stupid wisdom could not stay
His going so
the wanting never ended.

Drought

Water is no cause for sorrow;
our fate, our non-abiding,
is only rainbow or a summer snow
or melt of our after-loving.

Sorrow for the desert torpor,
old men pacing reason's cage,
yearning for lust or war
to freshen their furies; any rage
to tell them why, where, who they were
before the flood.

Poor Tom

Poor Tom remembers boy places,
faces of boyhood folk, old talk
where no sad clock trick-tocks his dream.
If Heart could just redeem its losses,
buy him back the brave sublime
he lost at dice to huckster time.

Poor Tom, for aye the Soul repeats
its wrecks, its losses, old defeats,
desperate, adrift, will cling
to some old, mis-remembered thing.

No settled scene

for Lisa

Memory has no settled scene
but reconfigures love and loss
as waters go from blue to green
to crystal clear forgetfulness.

Traveller

Belfast, Glasgow of the dismal rains!
Pilgrims have no human law
to right our loneliness; lit window panes
promise no redress nor welcome, only the raw
discourtesy of strangers.

Pilgrim, trailing through the sleet,
gale, snow, the roads lie open, if unsigned;
how many immortals did you fail to greet,
not decrypting their disguises, find
your ways obstructed by the sphinx? Do not try to cheat
her. You are the riddle's answer, bitter-sweet.

Capriccio: Puddle

Between wood-edge and plough the track ambles uphill
until, turning by the pines, it levels out where
there, after the rains, is a Puddle, not
what you call beautiful, cloudy red-brown, nor profound
or persistent enough to settle on clear reflection,
a guddle, superficially sensitive to skies,
muddle of earth and water – but never step in!
Puddle is home; summer water-boatmen, bugs
trudge its terrible meniscus – and at Puddle's edge, hint,
glint of a rainbow, where it bends into being Not Puddle.

To those busy with great matters, the patters
of politics, philosophies, urgencies of cash,
Puddle is vague, barely a memory
printed on earth. Even so, how can you not sense
Puddle is what makes the difference?
What surfaces in Puddle would astonish you;
a great gold moon, a Hokusai moon, tethered to
immortal pines black-silhouetted on a double sky,
and in the dancing shallows between Puddle and time,
creatures, noises, delicately prancing deer, lightning, snow;

whin, rowan, broom, dog-rose and hazel come and go,
crows caw, the pheasants croak, the harebells chime.

Without my poor colour-of-rabbit-fur Puddle,
would be no presence for you to ignore.

Dawn

Heart, do you hear the small birds start
the dawn, vermillion, gold and green:
what lark says to the field, sky, hedge,
mole says to earth, vole to the water-sedge;
Heart, do you hear the small birds start?

If I climb high enough

If I climb high enough, Voirlich or Cruachan,
lie dead among dwarf juniper, mosses, lichen
on a moon-bare summer evening, stare
up into an utterly clear
heaven, I see, after the dizziness
and processional stars possess
the sky, a recession of blues go
through cornflower, cobalt, indigo
seamlessly mocking my
shades of infinity.

Birthday

Now in my summer time,
long enough in tooth, claw, rhyme
I praise the early whin and broom
gilding gold my other room;
until the bluebell and the may
put out their flags for my birthday.

The Ages of Water

1

I stoop to pluck one pebble from the tide,
wet-cool, white surfaces reflect the sun,
the shy waves hiss and smooth untidy sand,
isosceles sails trim the horizon:
whispers of air and water, shreds of cloud,
the footloose dune, cool smoothness in my hand,
salt breeze on skin, the body's pressing weight,
breath, heartbeat, steady brilliance of the light.
Mind is haunted by itself, thought-
phantoms, feeling-ghosts, rise, break, recede,
pale wisps of a wandering sea-mist,
unspoken gestures of a restless blood,
ghosts always with us in a present-past,
the weird intelligence that shapes a soul.

2

Whatever may pass
before it, the mirror
does not bear grudges.
Peer too close;
breath smudges
the glass.

3

Sun-heated waters rouse a restive gale;
they kiss, embrace, he runs his hands through leaves,
rummages grasses; in passageways the trash-
cans rattle, as big warm droplets splash
the decking, vineyard, street, drenching the earth
in earth's desire as the battleship clouds close-in.
Forever strange, Mind is sensual,
its sense the presences of absent things,
memories, desire, imaginings.
Between arousal and soul no barrier
defines where out and in end or begin.
The summer squall moves on, in search of other
souls; the onlooker still disbelieves
how presence changes waters into wine.

4

The harbour still, the wee boats sigh,
lobster pots loom high
by tangles of blue net,
the beckoning bay, obsidian plate.

The voice that ventures out is mine,
or croaking seagull or the sea;
death will be a lost collection,
idioms only you can say.

5

Past Knowetap's disused winding wheel,
past hawthorn boundaries to Thinacre;
rabbit-cropped, a daisy-spattered space, shawl
laid out with flasks, sandwiches, juice; and tall
as boy grasses, reeds, thistle, Eden
of birches, rowan, broom, minnows to paddle for
in the luminous burn with jar and fingers in
landscapes ignorant of absences or sin.
Akropoloi crumble, reach for inhuman,
too human, godliness, order, deny
mad islands of happiness, water on stone:
below the surfaces, in waves a micron high,
tumble-surge the great raw tides of mayfly
mortality, ruin, desolation, pain.

6

Silvery skeleton birches shiver
and rime. Overhead the great pale river
floods the firmament with time.

7

Edge and epicentre you are horizon,
your nature is water, mutability
accepting, reaching out, how else could it be,
surrounding, shaped by and shaping the stone.
Not near, not far, you colour everywhere
in tenderness or fear, delight, despair,
rainbow and sea-haar, frost-flower, moon-grin,
your lustful physics fuse without-within.

I cannot see through the window you see through.
Still, here you have lighted, inside my horizon,
painting through your frameless window
new Fragonards, Brueghels, Cézannes.

8

From his angle of view
God's face does not show
in the mirror; all you see
is the light reflected.

9

I am everywhere in you, flowering desire,
under my hands your body takes new shapes,
as water is shaped-by-shapes a stream.
Who knows what body knows; the why, for whom
self delegates itself to otherness? My dreamscapes
build no monuments, my breathing space
is intimate geography, water and fire.
Mind is a stranger, haunted by mortal mess,
blood, seed and marrow, carnal tenderness,
it hankers for chastity. But body's lexicon
is life, a metaphysic all its own:
substance and the insubstantial, waters
and word in a mortal jar, and hungers,
secret wants, kisses that always taste of tears.

10

Why is the moon so beautiful
when she steals her light from the sun?
Beauty is indivisible.
Light is One.

Dublin

Ninety, half-blind, Sister Augusta keeps her inflexible routine,
each noon, distributing not daily bread
but tattie mash, cabbage, mutton stew in a billy-can,
sustenance and blessing, to see the needy fed.
        And if our days grow dark,
        what human days do not?

Master Makars

Glossy master tunnel-makar mole with delicate
pink snout and pink long-fingered hands, makes
his poems differently from me; turning his cognate
verses underground, all scent and sound, earthquakes
being his *métier*,

while

Music-master owl flute-flutes from leafy libraries,
sonatas, reading the score by moonlight, barely tweaking
the silences, live to glissandoing ironies,

while

Maiden mayfly out on a one-day, one-way trip,
searches her dizzy heights for love in a *rondeau redoublé*.

The tune would not play

Timing off and the fingering clumsy,
the chanter resisting; then, at my back,
some sudden presence though I dare not look.
Commanding, weightless fingers cover mine
subdue, seduce the tune, once, twice, again,
seven times, the *feadan* sweet as a thrush
in the morning singing. Then only the hush
of absence. Shouldering the pipes they play
their music, sweetness of welcome and praise,
exile, exaltation, sadness of losses,
swelling and ebbing, strong as the sea;
flood tide and ebb tide, the dark disarray,
pride and the pain of raw humanity.

A Grandmother

Snowdrops in the garden yesterday,
des perce-neiges;
I dreamed of you, forty years dead,
of reconciliation for a break
that never was;
only these little spears of loneliness
only irreparable loss.

Advice to a younger poet

Avoid in bed
those with:

        too much make-up
        too much eye-glint
        too much fuck-up
        always skint.

Avoid in print:

        no fuck-up
        no eye-glint
        won't shut-up
        no flint.

Behind closed eyes

Behind closed eyes my worlds wear
another guise, erratic sea.
Between clock-tide and tsunami
monsters and lovers rise, dripping desire,
rage, tenderness, authority and disappear
in a great splash of the unexpected.

Light as Air

You are very light, said he,
lifting me high
and kissing me. And I reply:
As are we all; one day
we shall shimmer clear away.

Phoenix and Unicorn

Loving till day turns back to day, fondest
each in the other's arms, enchanted bodies spirit
us away over our glittery Bifrost.
Young to us as Earth was new, the half-lit
dawning streets were still, promising heat,
wan moon through cloud, delicious ghost
haunting the blossom-littered street.

Love, if that by which we live and grow,
fed on romance, grows famine-thin,
phantom-spoiler of what's here, chasing its shadow
mirror-self. We follow its wisp-will
through dark woods, till Juliet and Romeo lie dead,
the streets fogged-in, the bitter truths untasted.

Though winter now, memory still splinters
light in its old, sad colours, its prison-prism glinters
too on Plato's promises; *the Beautiful, Good, True*,
the hopes, were real, and living through
those rainbow days, we saw, on journeys born
in innocence, a phoenix-fire, a unicorn.

The Roman Road at Gask

Gask Ridge is quiet. The birds are shy,
save for a rattled, raucous jay,
pheasants' *korrk-kok, kutuk-tuk.*
The quiet never quite complete,
the Earn, the plough-field, thick-set fir
reduce to persistent murmur
A9 trucks, farm tractors, chain saws
                     busy with purposes.

                  There are three silences,
none absolute: the little noises, stirs
of small-bird, rustle-breezes through the firs,
the rainy-drip-drips, mouse-bustle, bee-hustle.
        Then there is heart-whisper, shuffle-
brush on a muted drum, the drawn
breath-in, out-whisper antiphon,
faint-far chorale sustains the blood.

Last are the silences of God;
Earth on her pilgrimage,
orisons, corona songs,
                    time holding eternity's rage
in his long, strong arms,
                    busy with purposes.

No sound without silences.

All the accounts say:
                    wolf and bear, faun and satyr
are extinct or never were; the legions' signal fires are out.
You think, perhaps, there are no spirits left
to help or threaten us, extinct alike, benign, malign.
You are wrong; it is we they accompany, we reft
them from our hearts. Imagine you hear the legions'
        drum, a sign
of selves beyond our grasp, enigmatic, sovereign.

Other Silences

I

When hurdy-gurdy crowds, the lights go out,
the heart-thump ride-machines jolt

                         halt at a breathless chasm-
edge, the red pony roundabout
stops, the spasm
diminishes to a sigh: unstrung, the marionettes
sprawl where they lie

                      incapably free
of mundane anxieties, jaggy frets.

II

Then steals another silence,

                      an after-peace, when
collared dove-selves flutter down
from look-out perches to a common space
a placeless lek for presences
to coo while time drips timelessness
on human want, too frail, too thin
for any space from skin to skin.

III

Our death is all deaths; we die
to each other when each is least;
then must we love us each the other most:
remembering our dispensation-space
on hills, where light like world-weather falls
as plenitude, a gentle, rainy fullness-grace
before we go back to the mean small chills
    of all our ordinariness.

Though you are sitting beside me

Though you are sitting beside me watching
the sea-fall, secure in some corner
of each other's shell, our worlds cling
to their secrets, opening only forever.

Your horizon is other, your sense
inflected with affections, injuries
only your own. Your present tense,
two-letter shift from *is* to *was*,
makes *us* too lightly disappear.

How can a Twain be wholly One,
each with its only darling,
if, fast in our osmotic chain,
your soul-tides ride to another moon,
our hearts go round a different sun?

Not really me

There is a sleight of soul we know
deceives the looker-on within:
that lies, hypocrisies, cargo
of self-afflicting wrongs be
written off as: *lost at sea,*
       not really me.

He faced the ills

He faced:
the ills of adolescent arrogance;
confused infallibility, lust, rage,
his hopeless hurt;
he faced.
All done with now,
replaced
with all the arrogance of age;
confused infallibility, lust, rage...

Compass

As the needle swings north ever,
so does the Heart turn ever home,
and the ageing traveller
recognises mountain, desert, seas,
long journeys down their cryptic ways,
for cells of a bitter honeycomb.

Ages I

Still awake or awake again
when the moon is a coin
on a black lacquer screen,
the night is one long sigh
of silk, and the Way
a trickle of water-sound....

As Moon goes pale
at threat of day,
wisdom is knowing
your losses
are never far away.

Autumn

Oak-red, rust-plum, birken-gold,
the green days oxidise and fall
and all that hunger for the light
turns to irreparable cold.

Pilgrim

Saint or sage,
remember;
the purpose of pilgrimage
is to kill who you were.

From time to time

From time to time he sips at his coffee,
not because it is hot or he is poor,
but to spin out an hour in the café.
Company is what he comes for,
a vice he hides from his self-regard. Better
still if the customers are young, even if they
see him only as furniture.

Meantime they lead lives he imagines
rich in adventure, excitement, nights of love.
From time to time he glimpses their twins
in mirrors behind the bar, longs to remove
the mask age has him wear, the thinning hair,
the spotted skin, slack-pouched eyes no longer clear,
and silence the whispering within;
why did I not... so quick... so soon...

The tricks God plays

The tricks God plays forbid
the tiger to escape his ways;
did Oedipus know his purposes,
whither and whys of a scene
he neither chose nor understood?
What sanctifies the author's will
of still unwritten tragedies,
for Man who cannot be but Man?

Green Apple

For J. and L. Callahan

I was sitting under the tree in its saving shade,
eating it slowly, the green apple, to savour
its texture and roundness, coolness, juices, flavour
not come across before. And when I had had
all but the core, I threw it into the wild grass
and left. Looking back, wasn't that the moment when
he should have introduced himself? He let it pass,
having to come back later as a Christ in pain.

Past Present

The clouded bloom, pale purple on a plum
shades into tenderness and loss; the phantom
moth and flittering pipistrelle
solicit ghosts, complicit bluebell
woods remember a spring wood long ago.
Delight and woe, delight and woe;
wounds and the lilac reveries, all
shadows cast by the invisible.

Cherries I

Sky and the cherry branch
heavy with snow;
slowly winter's knot unravels,
slowly the days go,
the bed so
bare without you.

Michelangelo to Cavalieri

I lost the wee book you gave me:
  Michelangelo to Cavalieri.
It said desire, love, beauty are a shallow stream.
I thought I could wade across to you.
It said your beauty was a proof God IS.
I thought; so many garden promises!
And bodies, light modelled as marble!
But the apple is water, ungraspable flame.
I drowned in seas no ship can sail.

> More than metaphor
> water is liquid light, is life,
> light momentarily alive.

Ages II

Spaces between the words are
wide, wider than
Glen Etive, their scouring slide
glacial avalanche.

Separation
is what words are for.

As glaciers retreat

As glaciers retreat
scour mountain-glen, loch-deep
light has bleached
you so I can peep
through orbits where appetite
and world meet.

Cherries II

Braidings loose, the fabric in places bare
where you would sit reading; the dish we bought
by the seaside still on Grannie's dresser.
Years later I went back there, thought
to find it the same, but the hotel
was boarded, though the Cherries we sat beneath
watching the sea-fall were in foam. Histories we tell
ourselves, each other, shape the worlds we bequeath.

Rememberings die, meanings disappear.
Your image in its two dimensions
is a flat conceit; intensified attentions
know no clock-tick time, the when-where
of whatever we are knows only *before* or *after*, makes
of invisible *Us* a sense of sense.
And what remains, our unassigned inheritance,
flutters to earth as petal-flakes.

The old black rosary

The old black rosary that draws my tear,
dear were the hands that counted it,
often anon and kind the heart.

The hand that counts your days
has done, has counted you away
from us, grief-broken, apart.

Many recall your gentle speech, courtesy
that won friendships, not in Gigha
alone but in Mull and green Islay.

Generous of hand and heart,
lover of songs and poems, the old way
was never neglected while you lived.

Harpers and poets came from Kerry
and Boyne to salute you; none did you
leave empty-handed or dismayed.

My slim, bright hawk of the hill,
devout, a salmon in wisdom's pool
in Connacht of the quiet streams.

Dún Súibhne is sad without music,
that lovely place we so delighted in,
that now I cannot bear.

Christ of the hazels, you have picked the best
of the cluster, taken it from us
too soon. Is it so wrong to mourn a hairst?

Oh, rosary that provokes my tear,
I wince at being left behind when
he of the soft, dark eyelashes is gone.

Oh, rosary that provokes my tear,
let Mary guard me day and night,
behind, before, until I too may disappear.

Each is a first

Each is a first, an only and a last,
a frameless window on a cloud of dust
floats and sparkles on the vast.

River

for David Lawrence & Laura Mathews

I see you there in the Avon,
to your waist in the low, slow river,
half in tree-shade, the slippery brown-green
boulders under your feet, your too-white skin
light-spattered, high sun a hard glitter
through canopy. Your name
is nothing to minnows,
sticklebacks nibbling your toes
and the river, I think, still flows
there, much the same.

Bindings

Stitching the sheets together now, intent,
the light still good for late afternoon,
watching dust-motes dance in the day-slant,
gathering by gathering, immune to *might have been*,
dead critics, revisionary loves, phases of the moon,
assembling as many of my tumbles, dissembles
temples and stumbles, trembles, mumbles
as fugitive days allow:
sheaves for a signature, spars for a Holy Rood.

Reflections

Two buzzards turn on the water-sky,
inscribe no trace; their images draw
circles of a life's circumference
in circuits of a sun and moon:
bubble-bursts rise from an unknown
space, slow ripples chase a presence-absence
on the pool; my reflections shiver and go.

What does a life inscribe – circles in air,
image in water? In the lower Tay
the sands shift unpredictably;
a dream topography where
wrecks and vanished places linger on.
Our boundaries lie just upon the skin,
meniscus keeps us from the absolute.

The buzzards turn, the raptor cry
knife-hard, concise in purpose,
keeps its promise, ripples away
to the inaudible; they wheel, rise
buoyed on the invisible. The moving
thing beguiles the eye, misses the gravity,
the inner-scape, the ruffled light.

In carriage windows backed by night,
an image questions who he is, as though
reflection could resolve the mystery:
water wakes you, others shape you,
light reflects you as you trickle, flow, flush
ebb, ripple, well, spring, flood, cascade, rush...
without you is only dusty death.

Between remembering, desire and dream,
the walls grow thin: voices of delight, the dying,
past-futures from another room,
circumference I have become.
Desire is bound to the physical, a taste,
the sound of you, your weight, your smell;
delight, the invisible, measures your smile.

The things my poor hands cannot hold!
Love, water, light: who is the pool
I could drown in, desert well
to drink from, be miraculously healed
by tender tinctures, a medicinal tear,
for mortal miscontent a cure,
soul respite from a solitary cell?

Love is fantasy, the dullards cry,
bodily want and nothing more;
as if the body were not mystery
enough, those secret moons, those tides that roar
and wreck our little domesticity,
drowning our cargoes,
coracles in Corryvreckan.

What is there else but, being individual,
to hold the sense-bound soul in trust?
Four hands enlace a knotting spell,
deep dye earth-colours in another's eyes
weave rainbows of reciprocal desire,
the alchemies that humanise
mortality; desire as feast, as yeast, as quest.

Was Plato right; all histories are circular;
the songs, the wars, the witless kings?
Or Leibniz, rather, that the strings
that thrum eternal winds are sentience,
inventing boundaries, our Out and In,
where water and the light are one,
lovers for ever, buzzard and prey?

Low tide, the Tay breathes out a sigh;
high overhead the great wind-rivers drive
the cloudy planetary breath,
the circling rains, the droughts,
desire and death, cruelty, beauty,
bound in her sole circumference;
two buzzards turn on the water-sky.

What can the Makar?

What can the Makar with his lonely spark
illuminate; firefly in a gloaming wood?
The charge is absolute; a sanctuary art
impersonal of personality, to mark
this where, *this* when, *this* cast, and educate the heart.

The stage is Argos, Edo, Dunning, the repertoire;
lust, love, greed, rage, revenge or pride, the trope;
that roles live on though audiences disappear;
great characters, *l'Avare, le Misanthrope*
fleshed out with cunning Servant, Lover lost,
the pious Fraud, old Nurse to organise the tryst,
equivocating Lawyer, kindly Whore.

And the endless self-rehearsal, mumbling over
what has to be said, bizarre reversal;
love lyrics muttered to the tone-deaf dead,
until in ultimate surrender, all we thought we were
collapses in earthquake and metaphor.

Herakleitos
for Michael Kincaid

Plagued once with youth as now with age, I dream
in memory so clear, soul aches
to step in her mountain stream

Fine age is ripe

Fine age is ripe, but mildly so,
not sickly sweet nor bitter,
nor so sour it spites its face, nor
greatly salt. Rather, with *parmigiano*
and green figs, coffee and grappa,
watches the gloaming *passeggiata*,
all ages dressed in their public best,
arm in arm, circle the piazza; this late
and passing throng we're here to celebrate.

Ragamuffin

Weary with prescience the ragamuffin
Soul knocks at the gate with crystal
bowl, soliciting his meagre keep, some wine,
food, shelter, mostly just someone to see him.

Old Man Mad with Poetry

The sun will shine for ever,
skies be ever blue,
youth last and love and life endure.
So dance, drink, play the night away,
the life so long, the love so true –
swifter than lightning in mirror-glance,
lighter than jenny-wren feather.

The old man glimpses the boy
through veils of chilling rain,
asserts through his regret, grief, pain;
suffering does not cancel joy.

Age

To stitch by stitch unpick
the tapestry we wove,
belief, skill, trick,
see what is left to save.

Senex

Morning scatters patchwork gold
on doors, floors, walls,
spatters his cabinets, falls
just anywhere, insolent, bold.

He fetches cloths and brushes,
rushes in a sad distress
to wipe the mess
from all His Things.

Earth not large enough

It is not Death should devil
me with fears and frights, frivolity
of scythe and skull, a sexless angel
or eternal pain; the mystery.
is life and Earth not large enough to hold us all,
so many demon-angels on a pin.

Marie Stuart

for Michael Granger

J'étais reine couronnée de France,
je suis, par Dieu, la reine d'Écosse,
ended the feast, the courtly dance,
the queen of loss.

No loss nor bitterness shall blot
my soul; their prudent treason,
triumph of all I am not;
my son, my barren cousin on her throne.

Betrayed by sex and by my heart,
I loved the beautiful, the false, the weak;
no mortal man is set apart.
How soon they break!

Weak, so I loved and weaker lost,
cut out my heart, cut off my head!
Cheated of life I pay the cost;
they will not cheat me of my God.

Words

Not friends, though you wish them innocent,
nor your agents, they do not labour
on your behalf, but conspire an ancient
treason, having no blood of their own to shed.
They guide you darkly, whisper who you are,
name you, wed you, bury you.

Love-matches between word and thing,
miscegenation, old beyond imagining:
they will lay the charges, judge and jury,
they will convict you.
Those you coffin on the page
will not lie quiet with the dead.

Before we were, they whispered in bed,
shouted in grief, loneliness, rage,
groaned in pain or prayer for the dead:
> *Through the golden veins of language*
> *runs the sullen, passing flood;*
> *lust and tenderness, despair, a stage*
> *where angels wrestle in the mud.*

Plea for a Healing

Long this enfeeblement, this lack.
All the fat cattle of Munster, the black
sturdy cattle of Scotland I would give to be well,
if I had them, even the great bull of Cuailnge
to be out again on the hill
hale and watching a summer's dawn and see
the new sunlight washing Glen Artney.

As fee for my healing I would give
the high white horses of Manannan, sportive
and brisk; the trumpets of Fionn,
the spear of Cu Chullain, all to be well,
if I had them, out with my love on the hill
at day's ending, and Voirlich limned by the sun.

The shield of the king of the Sidhe,
harp that brings sleep to a darkening soul,
I would pay gladly to be well.
Time unrelenting as the sea
has struck me hard; the wound is mortal;
white spray lies heavy on me, blazon
of snows over ice on Sgurr nan Gillean.

All these goods I would give and gladly to be well,
if I had them, but poor and feeble
now, have nothing to give for my bargain with time,
nothing but words and a rhythm, a rhyme.

Before the Javelin

We stand each on the deepest reach
of time, spine of the last mountain,
source-destination,
silence giving birth to speech.

When all fear fades, what but an *I*
proclaims the indescribable sky,
names lunar seas, Antarctic dawns,
leptons, leprechauns, black swans,
dew-dotted song-webs hung about histories?

Then in that poise,
that ever-lasting still
before the javelin,
balancing body-mass against the pull,
I measure my thankfulness,
rolling the world under my tongue.

Dark Times

Best, like Akhmatova, secrete a carapace,
reviled by hacks and model citizens would shove
you to death, or praise when they want you
for what you swore they would not have.
That moment past, safely reviled, be true
to your own insanity to rave, live, love,
a canny ghost haunting their sad disgrace.

In China

In China they say;
in the moment of death
you may, in the exhalation
of that unreturning breath,
just glimpse the soul-bird rise away,
snow-white, as a slow-winged heron.

After Death

How can I forgive?
You left no place to live,
no destination,
only a gloaming helplessness.

Who else to talk to but the dead?
Who else so slowly wise and sane?
Who else will listen patiently
never argue back, complain?

After-Life

That pathos of domestic things
after our lives abandon them,
that creaking stair a requiem.

Epitaph

after Lucian

They weave their spells around you –
    all things pass away.
Not so! We go. They stay.

Redemption

I.M. Isabro Ortega

Carving, with a small sharp blade,
I undercut a chin, scrape hollows
for cheeks, groove finely the forehead,
shape deep crevasses round a nose.
Gouge, scrape, turn; the holes are eyes;
mouth is the hardest, slow, slow
is the carving of speech until the wood says: *Rise,*
forget your loss, there is a magic to be made

If you fall

If you fall I will catch you;
sesame opens the magic door
and over the threshold I tumble
into your silences;
red deserts tender-urgent
white snow-scapes in dream descent
fall-sink in black seas
where even the rivers forget who they were...
　　　　　but you catch me
　　　　　and we stumble
　　　　　safe to shore.

Seasons

Play springtime on the pipes of Pan,
hymn when the body wakes like dawn.

Let summer's poetry be song,
give lyric voice to right a wrong

and autumn's poetry be praise,
paean for friendship, fruiting days.

Winter's poetry should be peace;
elegy, eloquence, release.

NOTES

Methven Moss

Methven and Dupplin are within a few miles of Dunning: the battle of Methven Moss in 1306 was a major defeat for Bruce; Dupplin in 1332 was another defeat for the Scots at the hands of Edward Balliol. Strategic in relation to the Tay and the Earn, and so determining access to the north, in and around Dunning has been an important settlement site since at least the Bronze Age.

Deirdre & Naoise

In the Ulster Cycle, Deirdre of the Sorrows (*Deirdre an Bhróin*) is fated to love Naoise and the prophecy is triggered by a combination of black, white and red; Naoise's killing of a boar, the red blood, the white snow and the raven feeding. Their time of happiness is in Scotland before Naoise is lured back to Ireland to be killed and Deirdre to kill herself.

Marsyas

The Titian, circa 1575, which now hangs in the Archdiocesan Museum Kroměříž in Czechoslovakia, was his last completed work. The portrait by Titian - or his studio - of **Suleiman**, circa 1530-40, is in Vienna's Historisches Museum Gemaldegalerie.

Pulcinella

Is a traditional, hump-backed, long-nosed, hermaphrodite character from the Neapolitan *Commedia dell' arte*. He is the original of Mr. Punch as well as contributing to the character of Figaro.

Knowetap & Thinacre

Place names from around the South Lanarkshire village of Quarter. The great winding wheel for the mine at Knowetap was a prominent local sight of which nothing now remains.

Roman Road at Gask

Gask Ridge marks the northern rim of Strathearn. Agricola, in his brief campaigns around 80 AD, had a road built along it with a line of signal stations. Sections of that road can still be walked and the circular bases of a couple of the signal stations can still be seen.

The Old Black Rosary

The story is taken from the *Book of the Dean of Lismore*, put together in Glen Lyon in Perthshire in the early sixteenth century and containing material from both the Ulster and Fingalian cycles as well as later works, at a time when the cultural links between the west of Scotland and Ireland were still intimate. It is the lament of a wife for her husband, Niall Óg, chief of Clann Néill of Castle Sween and dates from the second half of the fifteenth century.

Marie Stuart

The Scottish queen and former queen of France was executed on the orders of her cousin, Elizabeth I, in February 1587. On the evening before, Mary was refused access to a catholic priest and subjected instead to a puritan diatribe. She was allowed to see the French ambassador.

Old Man Mad with Poetry

In old age Hokusai often signed his work *Old Man Mad with Painting*.

Plea for a Healing

The idea comes from a text in the Dean's Book, by an otherwise unknown Eóghan Mac Combaigh. The text also contains a reference to Fionn's magical drinking horn: "which turned the water with which it was filled in to sweet-tasting, delicious mead.".

Isabro Ortega

A gifted wood-carver in Truchas in New Mexico. As a young man he fell into drink and petty criminality until, one day, carving a figure, the figure spoke and told him his fate was to carve. He took over a two-storey house in Truchas and covered every surface; doors, joists, cupboards, bed with wonderful, intricate carving in traditional native patterns.

THE AUTHOR

Walter Perrie is a Scottish poet, editor, critic and publisher. He was born into a mining village in South Lanarkshire in June 1949 and after Hamilton Academy, worked for several years in the Burgh Library before removing to Edinburgh in 1970 to read for an M.A. in philosophy, to which he later added the M. Phil. from Stirling.

By the age of thirty he had won a Gregory award for Poetry and his first major book of poetry (A *Lamentation for the Children*) had won a Scottish Arts Council book award. He had also been co-founder, with George Hardie, of *Chapman* magazine and was playing an active part in Scottish literary life, having interviewed Hugh MacDiarmid and organised Scottish participation in the first International Cambridge Poetry Festival, represented by Duncan Glen, Donald Campbell and Sorley Maclean.

During the 1980s he travelled widely in Europe and North America, holding the post of Scottish-Canadian exchange fellow and was later writer in residence at the University of Stirling. At the same time he became managing editor of *Margin*, an international arts quarterly under the editorship of the American writer Robin Magowan. In 1988 he was the recipient of an award for his poetry from the Ingram-Merrill foundation and was later to meet and correspond with James Merrill and in 2017 to hold a Merrill Fellowship, living in Merrill's former home in Stonington, Connecticut.

In the late 1980s he moved to the Perthshire village of Dunning. In 1990, in the context of the collapse of the eastern bloc, he was to drive across eastern Europe to write *Roads that Move* and in 2000 was awarded a Society of Authors travelling scholarship. It was from Dunning that, in 2005, along with the Scottish novelist and short-story writer John Herdman, he founded *Fras* magazine and Publications and has gone on to publish over thirty books and pamphlets of Scottish letters, including interviews with Donald Campbell, Trevor Royle, Margaret Bennett and Alasdair Gray as well as twice-yearly issues of *Fras* magazine.

Perrie's literary interests have encompassed essays on W. H. Auden, Lord Byron, Hugh MacDiarmid, Edwin Morgan and Muriel Spark. He has translated some of the *Fables* of La Fontaine as well as poems by Jacques Prévert and continues to give French-language talks on subjects of Franco-Scottish interest.